Going to the Hospital

A TODDLER PREP™ BOOK

All proceeds from this book go to the
Mark Puder Research Lab at Boston Children's Hospital

Copyright 2023 ReadySetPrep LLC

Toddler Prep™, ReadySetPrep™, and associated trademarks are owned by and used under license from ReadySetPrep LLC.

All rights reserved. No part of this book may be reproduced or used in any manner without written permission of the copyright owner except for the use of quotations in a book review. For more information, contact author.

All characters and events are products of the author's imagination, and any resemblance to actual events, places or persons, living or dead is entirely coincidental.

Photo credits: © Shutterstock.com

About Toddler Prep™ Books

The best way to prepare a child for any new experience is to help them understand what to expect beforehand, according to experts. And while cute illustrations and fictional dialogue might be entertaining, little ones need a more realistic representation to fully understand and prepare for new experiences.

With Toddler Prep™ Books, a series by ReadySetPrep™, you can help your child make a clear connection between expectation and reality for all of life's exciting new firsts. Born from firsthand experience and based on research from leading developmental psychologists, the series was created by Amy Kathleen Pittman—mom of two who knows (all too well) the value of preparation for toddlers.

We're going to stay at the hospital. There will be lots of new things to see and do. Let's talk about what happens when we're at the hospital.

A hospital is a place where doctors and nurses take care of people. Some people stay for a short time, and others stay longer.

We spend the night when we need extra help from doctors and nurses.

When we arrive, we check in at the registration desk.

You get a bracelet or a badge with your name on it so everyone knows who you are.

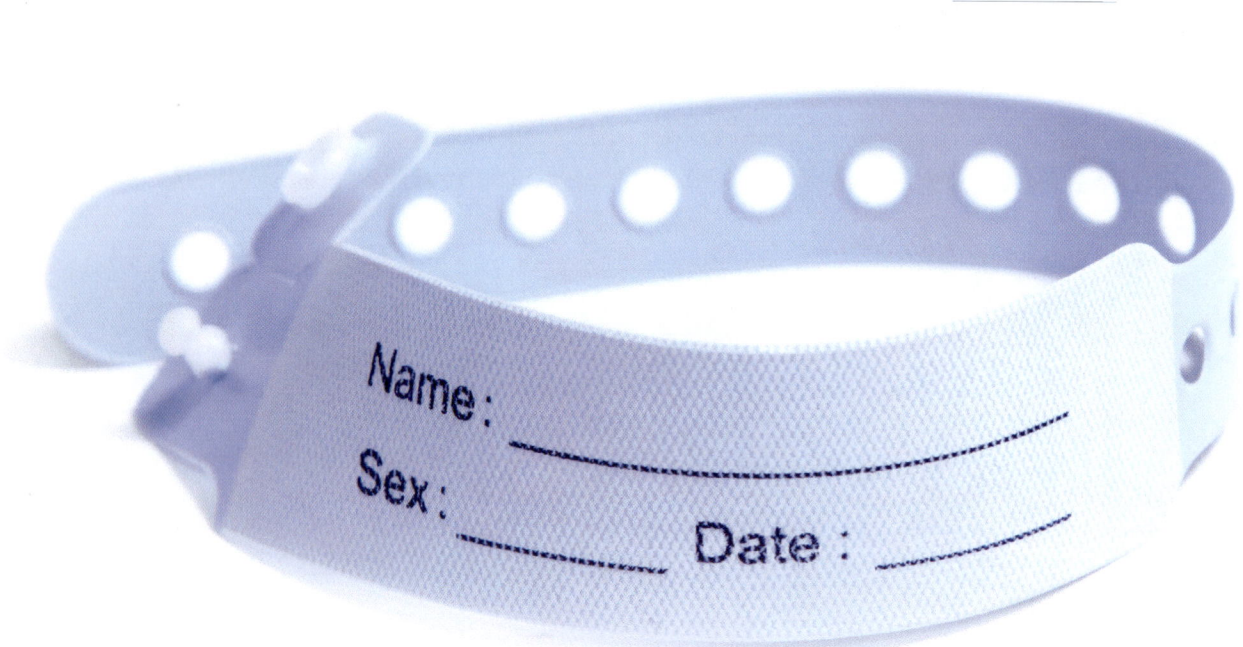

Then, a nurse takes us to our room. This is where we sleep and spend most of our time.

Sometimes, we share our room with another child who is staying in the hospital.

Inside the room, there is a bed for you to lie on, and tools for the doctors and nurses to use.

Next, you change into a comfy hospital gown. You can also play with the toys we brought from home.

Then, one of the nurses who will help us during our stay will come in to say hello. Their job is to make sure we are comfortable and have what we need.

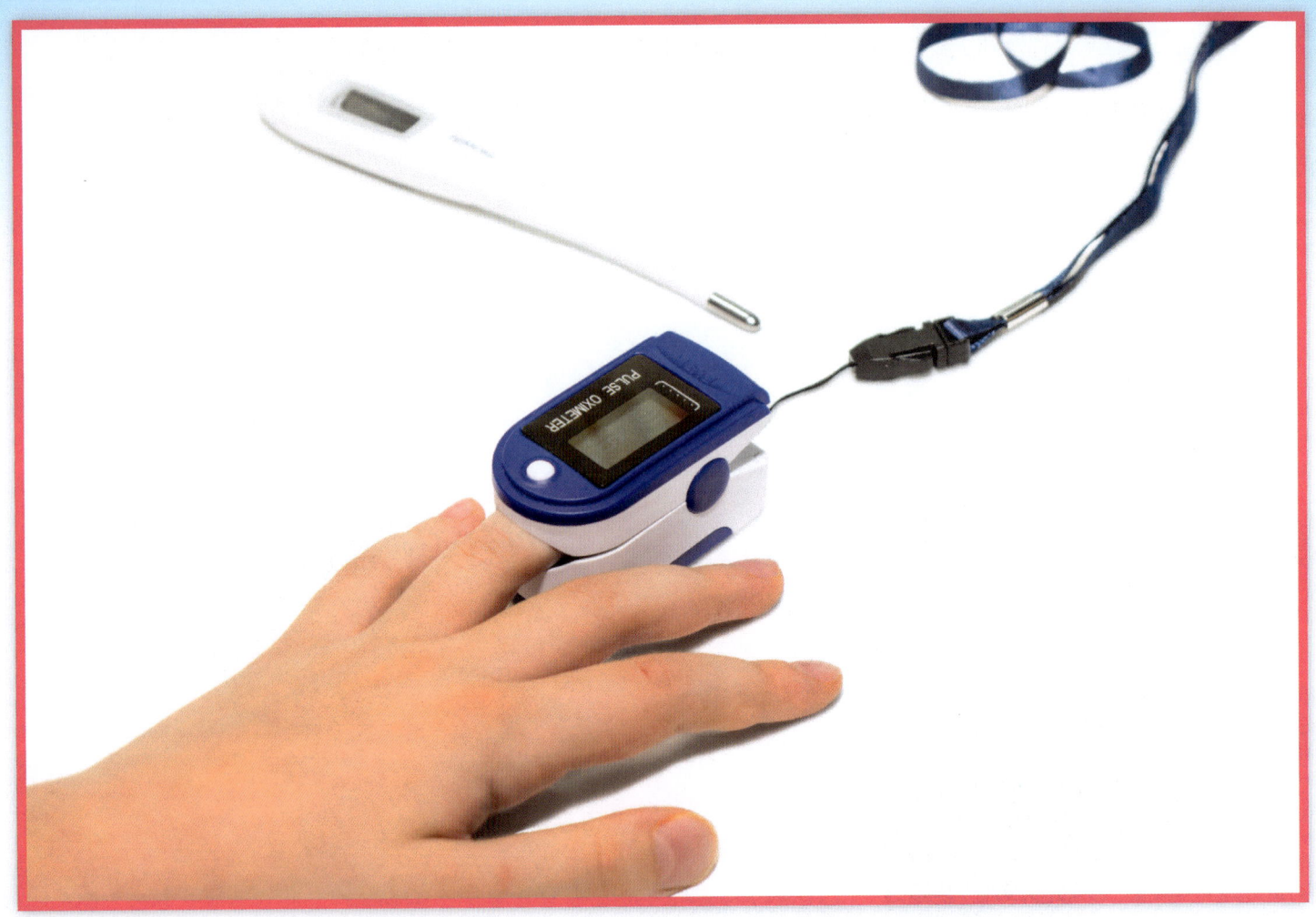

The nurse measures how tall and heavy you are. They also check your temperature, pulse, and blood pressure. These are called your vital signs.

The nurse checks your vital signs a few times each day and night. It may be different than what we're used to, but it doesn't hurt.

We see doctors each day we're at the hospital. They tell us what we need to do, and if we need any special medication, tests, or procedures.

Sometimes, the doctor visits our room with other people who are also part of our care team.

While we are in our room, we can read books, color, do puzzles, and play games.

When you feel hungry, we order food from the hospital cafeteria. They have sandwiches, fruit, and even dessert!

The food comes right to our room when it's ready. You can even eat in bed!

At nighttime, you sleep in your bed while I sleep beside you. You may hear the nurse come in to check on us, but you can go right back to sleep.

It's ok if you have more questions at the hospital. You can always ask me, the doctors, or nurses—everyone is here to help.

After you get all the help you need, the doctor tells us it's time to go home - hooray! We pack our things and say goodbye to everyone who took care of us in the hospital.

Printed in Great Britain
by Amazon